Caribbean Schools in Crisis

What is wrong in our schools today

Dr. Beverly Merrill

Published in 1998 by the Samuel Publishing Company Inc.

Copyright c 1998 by Dr. BEVERLY MERRILL

All rights reserved. No part of this book may be reproduced or transmitted in any form by any means, electronic or mechanical, including photocopying, recording or any informational storage or retrival system without permission in writing from the author or publisher.

ISBN Number 1-57087-422-0

First Edition

LIBRARY OF CONGRESS
Library of Congress Number 98-67147

Printed and bound in the United States of America
by Professional Press Inc.
P.O. Box 4371, Chapel Hill N.C 27515-4371
919/942-8020 Fax: 919/942-3094

Samuel Publishing Company, Inc,
P.O.Box 1206
St Johns, Antigua
West Indies
Tele/Fax: (268)462-6076
E-mail address: merrill@canw.ag

DEDICATED

to

My Daughters
Talitta and Tammy
whose encouragement, advice
and Teenage Wisdom
helped make this
book a reality.

Contents

	Introduction	vii
I	Teachers are fed up	1
II	Today's school problems are a reflection of societal chaos	4
III	Meeting the problem Head-on	25
IV	Fighting the problem	31
V	Effective School Discipline	37
VI	Promoting Better Student-Teacher Relationship	56
VII	The Successful Teacher	66
VII	Instructional Successful Schools	70
IX	Parents Involvement	81

INTRODUCTION

Many schools throughout the Caribbean are in serious crises. This calls for immediate attention and swift action. Dr. Beverly Merrill gives a precise analysis of the alarming state of our schools today. Caribbean Schools in Crisis not only expresses in brilliant detail what is happening but also sets a bold agenda to restructure our schools and reclaim our children from failure and indiscipline.

With Characteristic brilliance Dr. Beverly Merrill describes conditions which are leading to school failure. The impact of Cable Television and the Video world in the lives of our children, the rising rate of single parent household and sibling families, intellectual decline of our boys, the death of natural curiosity among our children, teaching methods which are no longer relevant to modern trends, Individualism and Isolation, Disesteemed teachers - the decline of the status of teaching as a profession in Western Communities. What can be done? asked a growing number of social commentators.

Dr. Merrill responds effectively with detailed yet precise solution to combat failure and indiscipline in our schools.

She calls for a regional accountability to teachers and Teaching. This book is a passionate cry to save our children. It is imperative reading for anyone who is in the business of loving children and saving our region.

A MUST FOR EVERY PARENT, EVERY EDUCATOR, EVERY LEADER

CHAPTER 1

TEACHERS ARE FED- UP

"I am fed-up with teaching....I don't feel good about myself anymore..."

"I really love teaching. This is what I've always wanted to do, but I am thinking seriously of changing my profession..."

"The pressure in teaching is too great. Lots of teachers are suffering from high blood pressure..."

"I have been teaching for thirty-five years. What do I have to show for it?"

"I don't know what's wrong with our kids today. It's so difficult to maintain control in the classroom...."

"What's wrong with our kids...."

"Education has gone to the dogs...."

"What's happening in our schools...."

"What's wrong?....."

LOSING YOUR WAY IN CLASSROOM CHAOS

Every burnt-out teacher was once an excellent teacher or an aspiring excellent teacher who lost his/her way in classroom chaos bureaucratic finger pointing and low pay. These educators lost sight of themselves, their teaching goals, enthusiasm and motivation. Tension, frustration and discouragement have become the nucleus of their job. They are caught in a vortex of classroom chaos, assignments, teaching and high blood pressure. Underpaid, overworked and unappreciated, they see themselves going in circles, getting nowhere as professional educators.

BECOMING A "MISTER CHIPS"

Almost every educator has become a kind of Mr. Chips. An unwanted relic of a past generation. An unrewarded persona non grata of an ungrateful system, a system which has moved rapidly with rapid changing of times, leaving teachers bewildered, exhausted and confused, searching for a common ground, searching for answers to make sense of chaotic classrooms, answers that would make their job a little less stressful, answers to the rising crescendo of bewilderment and helplessness........

"WHAT IS WRONG IN OUR SCHOOLS TODAY!"

Phenomenal social problems for the first time is creating unprecedented crisis in Caribbean schools. What are educators to do? What can the education system do to combat this crisis? Bewildered and despairing teachers complain that academic lethargy and lack of discipline in our schools have become epidemic. Some blame this on skyrocketing sexual activity among our young people, some on moral uncertainty, others on cable television, still others point to widespread disunity in our modern family unit. While educators are left to search for the prescriptions to our school crisis.

CHAPTER 2

TODAY'S SCHOOL PROBLEMS ARE A REFLECTION OF SOCIETAL CHAOS.

THE WEAKENING OF FAMILY BONDS.

Increasingly, we see phenomenal destabilization of children generated by dysfunctional families. The weakening and breakdown of family bonds have created isolation and conflict within the family system.

In the last twenty years the Caribbean has witnessed not only the rapid disintegration of families but also the changing of the family structure. The terminology 'family' has lost its traditional definition of a household of adults and children and have been placed under more elaborate sociological definition to embrace more widespread classifications.

With discomfort we see the rise of the sibling family, often a dysfunctional unit. Its older members no more than children themselves are left to assume responsibility for their younger siblings. In some of our more advanced communities, the extended family has disintegrated. Grandmas and grandpas have become relics of antiquity, throw-aways of communities bustling with civilization and are packed into nursing homes. They are no longer on hand to create feelings of stability social cohesion and security through a sense of continuity to our youngsters. Sadly, we view our elders as economic and social burdens while we shamelessly discard them.

SINGLE PARENTS ON THE INCREASE

Although the matriarch household is a cultural truth of the Caribbean, divorce and separation however have increased the percentage of single families.

There are psychological issues which pervade every aspect of the single parent's life and these issues affect their sense of self. Most single mothers are women with children whose fathers have either abandoned them physically or emotionally. At the core of the personality of the single mother is a sense of rejection and betrayal, a feeling of having been used and abandoned. This perception in large part may help govern her self-esteem as a woman and to a great extent dictate her attitudes towards her children. It takes a tremendous amount of psychological energy to maintain a home and raise a family single-handedly. Added to that are stresses of the job plus hormonal or chemical problems. Many single mothers live on the verge of psychological explosion. Most of them have nowhere to turn to for help and sadly their children bear the brunt of their frustration.

TWO TYPES OF PARENTS

Some adults are ill-equipped to be parents, while others have nurturing personalities and enjoy being parents:

1. *The sperm dona.* This type of parent gives birth to children but is incapable of nurturing them. Although they may take care of their material needs they are unable or unwilling to give emotional fulfilment. Such parents are likely to be emotionally distant.

2. *The nurturing parent.* This type of parent might be a biological parent or assume guardianship of a child. Such persons have nurturing personalities. They are capable of giving love freely. Both men and women fall into either one of these categories. *The sperm dona* may pose psychological danger to the child such as child abuse, rejection and abusive or permissive parenting style. Many such parents dispense with their responsibility of nurturing through material trinkets and indifference. Many expect educators to address and rectify this societal phenomenon. Teachers try to correct parent's mistakes but they too are confused and frustrated. Where they attempt to discipline, parent's complain. The sad irony is that parents

A REFLECTION OF SOCIETAL CHAOS

expect them to mould, shape and nurture their children and yet complain when teachers set out to do precisely what they are expected to do.

CHILDREN ARE NOT REARED, THEY ARE TURNED LOOSE.

It is an undeniable fact that "Undisciplined children make impossible students".

Today's Caribbean parents rear children arbitrarily by trial and error. For the most part children are not reared, they are turned loose.

Most family unit lack guidelines relevant to modern trends. Children need to be moulded, nurtured with love and discipline. They need to be given a goal orientation, and moral values within the family structure if they are to become efficient students.

Parents who by necessity and moral obligation should be their children's first teachers are faltering lamentably in that task. The energy of today's family focusses on its economic survival and permissiveness or don't-care parenting style. Too often the results are children with low levels of motivation and lack of discipline.

SUPPORT SYSTEM

The widespread breakdown of the family structure has created a growing dependence on peer support systems. Adolescents give advice to adolescents. Their wisdom and dialogues are based on their perceptions which have a limited range of experience. Consequently, they are incapable of guiding each other to a state of healthy maturity. In numerous instances it is a case of the blind leading the blind.

INTERGENERATIONAL CONFLICT

Educators are confused by students thriving on a wave of ideologies totally different from the ones they know. They are not faced with the traditional intergenerational conflict or gap. The battle is more frightening, more overwhelming. It is not the battle of the unacceptability of hairstyles, slangs and dress codes. If this was the problem it would be relatively easy to handle but this is a deeper battle, a more dangerous one where the basic formation of students is alien to Adults' Nature.

The socio-psychological explanation for this old age adult-child conflict can no longer be centred on growth sprout and hormonal imbalance. Today, this singular explanation is too simplistic, too narrow.

RELATIVITY OF TRUTH

Present day Caribbean teachers are faced with a generation of students who subscribe to an international youth culture which in turn subscribes to circular humanism and the relativity of truth and not to the universality of values. Their concept of truth as being an individual experience is one of the strongest aspect of their moral postulate. The era of a universal rightness and wrongness of behaviour, thoughts and attitudes has become an incredulous or laughable concept. A feeling state (what makes me feel good is good for me) is the predominant philosophy which governs our young people's moral and ethical concerns.

Some contend that our modern day students are a lost generation shuffling sideways, backwards, without a public vision.Teachers are overwhelmed by their students foreignness. They simply cannot cope, neither can they subjugate their value system to their students' dangerous new philosophy. **What are they to do?** They have no guidelines relevant to modern trends.

THE DEATH OF CURIOSITY

We have witnessed the death of natural curiosity, the thrill of knowing, the love of the acquisition of knowledge. the libraries used to be a meeting place where one poured over the great thinkers, the excitement of "Plato's Republic" and Aristotle. One wanted to know them, to live them, to breathe them. They moulded our intellect, shaped our vision and helped our moral destinies. Modern youth seeks to acquire knowledge to pass exams...barely. They demand so little of their vast potentials.

EDUCATION HAS LOST ITS MORAL OBJECTIVE

There was a time when the three R's were taught as academic rudiment to the greater traditional goal of moulding and cultivating the humanness of the individual.

In the confusion of being faced with a confused restless generation of students. Education has lost its traditional goal. In classroom which are no more than war fields, battles of wills are being fought and superficial knowledge attempted to be imparted by exhausted, overburdened, underpaid and discouraged educators.

OVERCROWDED CLASSES

Today's exhausted teachers, pressured by over-crowded classrooms, parents and education boards teach for the sole purpose of achieving passes. Schools compete for the highest on academic passes on exams, consequently in given situations, teachers miscalculate and blunder miserably. Many children who do not perform well at a given point in time have their future jeopardized by anxious pressured educators. Scaled to academic levels lower than their potential, they are prepared for a lowered level exam or eliminated from the exam so as to protect the school from the stigma of failure. The race of education is not towards looking at the child as a whole person but gaining the highest number of academic passes on the regional exam. The education system harassed by overcrowded unmotivated unruly classes has lost its moral objectives which used to be the production of responsible successful citizens.

THE IMPACT OF CABLE TELEVISION ON OUR CARIBBEAN YOUTHS

"Women who watch X-rated movies, do they get horny?" asked an eleven year old of his older brother. "Does a woman have to go to a bar to get a man?" Why do men love to suck a woman breast?"

These are just some of the questions which pervade the minds of our young television viewers. In the past twenty years cable television has impacted enormously on the Caribbean. It's influence is incalculable. It has become our greatest source of national and regional entertainment. Our Caribbean children are being indoctrinated into the world of television at an early age. Children's minds are sensitive and responsive to environmental stimuli and cable television has become the most potent stimulus in moulding their minds. Without our conscious knowledge an entire generation of our youths are being reared by this electronic device. Their ambition is being moulded by the television and video world. The danger is that cable television is not rooted in traditional values which is necessary to give a sense of rootedness, a sense of belonging and a sense of cultural identity. Most of the shows presented to our children are shallow, and project a distorted presentation of human social behaviour and a vastly erroneous perception of adult life. Profanity in movies have become preponderant. In addition, the average television family is disruptive. Television children portray a high degree of disrespect to their parents.

Children pattern their moral codes, values and beliefs on environmental influences. The messages embedded in uncensored programme-content are bound to have a negative impact on their pliable minds. Our children's minds become nullified with the acceptance of casual sexuality, immediate gratification, the acceptance of disruptive behaviours. Every year, thousand of our children with defect reality orientation are being sprued into the classroom. What are educators to do? This generation of teachers are the first ones to witness a

A REFLECTION OF SOCIETAL CHAOS

phenomenal decline in motivation, and self-discipline and an upsurge in widespread cognitive lethargy. Such academic lethargy and intellectual passivity are unprecedented when compared to students of previous generation.

Numerous studies have been conducted on the impact of television on the minds of children. These studies revealed that excessive television viewing results in incalculable damage. These damages fall on a wide spectrum and range from confusion over moral standards, the imitation of antisocial acts, the obsession with sexual perversion to severe damages done on cognitive skills.

A 1987 STUDY

Studies on the effect of excessive cable television viewing on the youngsters cognitive and academic performance revealed that "too much television too early produces academic passivity, day-dreaming, a limited attention span" and the systematic erosion of creative imagination.

A 1987 study conducted by the Author (Merrill '87) to determine the impact of cable television viewing on the academic performance of Caribbean students found that excessive television viewing reduces academic achievements and motivation to an alarming extent and promotes "learner frustration".

It is observable however that throughout the school system educators come into contact with mental apathy or mental passivity in the classroom. Many of our youngsters are reluctant or afraid to meet new challenges, to accept the frustration inbuilt in learning and to plough on with tenacity. Such children are often a despair to conscientious educators.

The author has and continues to encounter a disproportionate number of children who portray little or no creativity, imagination and initiative and whose comprehension of abstracts is so inadequate, it is alarming.

The 1987 study revealed that many High School aged television viewers regard school as disinterested and a waste of time. This perception of school is more prevalent among Second and Third Formers. Respondents who watched television late complained of sleepiness in the classroom. They exhibited a tendency towards mental apathy and lack of learner motivation.

In a follow-up study, letters were dispatched to parents urging them to monitor and reduce their children's viewing. The youngster's concentration level increased markedly. They had better comprehension of abstracts and they engaged to an observable degree in behaviours which require initiation and effort.

15 A REFLECTION OF SOCIETAL CHAOS

Research findings established conclusively that excessive television viewing has a negative impact on the Caribbean child's cognition and level of academic motivation.

ISOLATION AND INDIVIDUALISM

Caribbean people used to be closed knit. A woman once saw it her right to discipline another woman's child. Today's neighbours no longer know each other. Communities are divided not by structural boundaries but by boundaries of coldness and indifference. Our people have become increasingly individualistic and young people are left much to their own devices.

THE WIDENING OF THE ECONOMIC GAP

The capitalistic greed, selfishness and tunnel vision of a lopsided western economy as well as mismanagement from some Caribbean governments have created increased national poverty and economic destitution for the average person. We witness the domino effect in family conflict, male gender apathy and withdrawal, female gender frustration and academic lethargy and deviant behaviours in our youngsters.

Economic and social destabilization on a national level results in economic and social destabilization within the family unit which in turn creates destabilization of its young members and this in turn creates tremendous problems in the school system.

WOMEN FORCED OUT OF THE HOMES

The advent of the woman's liberation movement deromanticized the traditional belief of the woman's place in the home. A sense of irresponsibility among some of our men, economic stagnation, divorce, increasing matriarchal headed homes have forced many women out of the homes and into the work-place resulting in less supervision for children, less time and energy to rear them. Of course, there are students who are surviving healthily in spite of our social malaise but increasingly, large numbers of them are suffering and educators meet them in the classroom... insolent, impulsive, argumentative, chaotic, confused, lethargic and insensitive. They have a deflated perception of education. Education is perceived as a force upon horror and not a real or practical need. On a day to day basis, educators witness an upsurge in resistance to education. Consequently, the average teacher is unhappy with teaching. They feel they are not making a contribution and their sense of commitment declines as they plummet into burnt out syndrome.

A REFLECTION OF SOCIETAL CHAOS

WAYWARD BEHAVIOUR

Children no longer experience consequences for wayward behaviour. It is through consequences that a social and moral conscience develops. In many of today's homes, wayward behaviour has become more of a norm or tolerance than an unacceptable deviance. Daily, confused and bewildered parents practise with incredible panache dysfunctional parenting styles. Family instability, couldn't-care-less parenting style will logically snowball into the school system.

AFFLUENT TEENAGERS

We live in an era of affluent teenagers. While parents struggle to provide basic essentials, they ascertain their teenagers have designer clothes, designer shoes, personalised television and telephone. Children take their affluent lifestyles for granted. Everything is so readily available.

Modern day children have no memory of an age of sacrifice, priorities and delayed gratification. A child's character takes formation based on his or her domestic lifestyle. If things are readily at hand, immediate gratification is built into the psyche. This transforms into impatience lack of self control and the belief that others owe them something. If things are delayed and worked towards systematically, one learns patience and the philosophy that hard work leads to accomplishment, Self-control is learned and internalized through delayed gratification. But today's parents attempt to give their children everything. Unwittedly, parents are denying their children viable opportunities for the development of self.

Today's Caribbean parents deprive children of attaining the very fibres that moulded their character into the remarkable men and women that many of them turned out to be. They placed their children into an age of Aladdin's lamp with an effortless rub, all wants and need spring immediately and automatically. In their eagerness to protect their children from the hardship of life and to give them everything that they never had they over-indulge them.

One hears incredible reports of parents doing school projects or their children's domestic chores. This type of pampering is dangerous and defeating to our youngsters. it inhibits the developmental of confidence in one's ability and a sense of social responsibility. These are character building blocks that are learned in the home through responsibilities and not half-hearted lectures. Character training is vital. It transforms itself into self-discipline, goal orientation, motivation, planning, organization. All these are prerequisites for highly motivated and disciplined students.

OUTDATED TEACHING METHODS

In the classroom educators are confronted by a generation of children born into an age of rapid technological innovations. Television, one of this century's most influential technological devices has transformed Caribbean students into a visual generation. Traditional teaching methods which are audio-visual have been rendered archaic in today's classroom. Teaching methods have not kept up with rapid changes.

Increasingly, Caribbean youths are developing a visual preparedness for learning. Through excessive television viewing the eye-brain coordination is being trained to absorb learning to a greater extent than an ear-brain co-ordination.

A LOOK AT THE INFRASTRUCTURE

The rising rate of illiteracy and widespread discipline problems make it imperative for Education Boards to review the need for smaller classrooms. Smaller classrooms would create greater opportunity for closer supervision of students.

THE VALUE OF EDUCATION

Education is no longer esteemed as it once was. Part of the

reason some contend is that teachers are poorly paid and the teaching profession is a dying profession. Whatever the reason, it is an inarguable fact that education and modern day teachers in the Caribbean are poorly esteemed.

Education was once viewed as the gateway to a better socio-economic life, and therefore, in many Caribbean communities, income, job opportunities and professional upward mobility once reflected educational standings. Today, this is no longer the case. Emphasis and appreciation are placed heavily on technical skills. Job demands and financial restitution reflect that appreciation. Some of our young people do not see the relevance of an academic education in terms of their material betterment. Materialism and a practical mind set have also made the acquisition of an education for aesthetic purposes a disbelieveable concept.

Each year many of our young people enter the job market unable to read and write. Functional illiterates, they have not even mastered the basic academic skills. Society must create and emphasize avenues whereby education becomes a viable incentive to upward material mobility. All concerned parties must engage in a regional campaign to upgrade teachers and teaching.

A REFLECTION OF SOCIETAL CHAOS

OUR BOYS IN CRISIS

Currently the Caribbean is witnessing a socio-educational decendency of its adolescent and teenage boys. The widespread portrayal of intellectual lethargy and academic impotence is unprecedented in the History of the Caribbean. This state of affairs will doubtlessly have alarming consequences for our dispora.

Are our social institutions unwittedly programming our boys for psychological and academic retrogression?

The problem and solution are as complex as they are interwoven.

Essential elements of a 1996 observational study (Merrill '96) highlighted the following findings:

A spiralling percentage of adolescent and teenage boys are:

(1) more susceptible to the drug culture than girls.

(2) Get suspended from school more frequently than girls.

(3) Get into disciplinary problem.

(4) View school and education as a waste of time to a greater degree than girls.

(5) live in household with fathers who are either physically absent or emotionally distant.

(6) Want to get into the technical skills but do not see the relevance with a formal education.

(7) are less focussed, less goal-oriented than girls and are more likely to drift into lethargy.

(8) Require more structure and discipline than girls.

(9) are uninvolved in the vital processes of human social development.

(10) Engage to a greater degree in non-productive and destructive activities.

(11) Fewer boys than girls participate in extra-curricula activities such as typing and computer skills. Acquisitions which are essentially academic and career oriented.

A REFLECTION OF SOCIETAL CHAOS

(12) More adolescent and teenage boys are lured by the street and video arcades. The values of these institution are structured on the psychological symptoms of failure i.e. immediate gratification, sense experience, sexual permissiveness, drugs, exploitation, clothing, cars, get rich quick schemes, breaking the law, imprisonment and remaining unrehabilitated.

(13) Result of psychological profile in a clinical setting found that disturbances such as Autism, Attention Deficit, Hyperactivity disorder (ADHD) were noticeably more prevalent in adolescent and teenage male patients than female patients. These disorders seriously impede learning.

(14) In the Nursery and lower primary grades boys and girls achieved academically at the same rate. There is no difference in level of confidence, enthusiasm and motivation. In high school academic behaviour assume a sharp difference. Enthusiasm and motivation transform into apathy in a higher percentage of boys as compared to girls.
The 1996 observational study also reveal that girls in the

higher primary and High School grades outdistance boys in linguistic competence and flexibility of mind.

(15) Teenage girls are more likely to be hired during vocation and after school in jobs which demands academic aptitude such as library, lawyer and doctors offices. Girls are supervised to a greater extent than boys. Their energies and activities are more structured and channelled in areas which promote academic and psychological development.

(16) The responsibility of such religious and social activities as Sunday School teacher, choir member, club coordinator are more likely to be given to teenage girls.

(17) Psychological profile in a clinical setting showed that female drug takers show less aggression and paranoia than boys.

CHAPTER 3

MEETING THE PROBLEM HEAD-ON

COPING IN TODAY'S CLASSROOM

Students come into the classroom with different personalities and different reasons for being there. They come from various backgrounds, with different habits, likes and dislikes. Some come unprepared to handle the demands of self-discipline and structure that the academic world demands. Some come from nurturing homes while others are victims of permissive or abusive parenting styles and they enter the school with dysfunctional social behaviours. Each classroom is made up of a continuum of different students. The ideal one on one end of the spectrum and the impossible students on the other end.

UNDERSTANDING THE IMPOSSIBLE STUDENT

It would be a fallacy to assume that every student wants to learn, Some impossible students are products of technological entertainment. They want to be entertained; they are unable to cope with the discipline and structure that school imposes.

Consequently, they find school dull and boring. They hate being there. They are there because they have no choice; they feel pressured by parents and societal dictates. For some of these students school is an escape from domestic crises or difficult abusive parents. They come to school reluctantly and keep their eyes on the clock. Teaching these students have become a classic case of taking the horse to water and attempting to make it drink. Teachers get the impression that these students think they are doing the teachers a favour just by being present in the classroom. They think educators are too demanding. They want to be left alone. Lacking motivation, they view the world as owing them something.

Impossible students are always on the defensive. They perceive school as a battle ground. They have developed an 'us against them' type of fighting mentality. Teachers are viewed as the enemy. When a teacher enters the classroom, impossible students expect trouble. They expect to be picked on, humiliated and rejected. They become confrontational. As a result, they usually have a negative relationship with teachers and a negative perception of school. They feel uneasy in the school setting. They have poor work ethics and they complain constantly.

Impossible students have a negative perception of themselves. They suffer from a low self-esteem. They are vulnerable to criticism. They are defensive and insecure. Some impossible students are actively involve in sex. Early sexual activity takes a young person's mind from obedience and compliance to a premature stance of an adult posture.

GIFTED STUDENTS

Students have differences in learning rates. Some students assemble concepts at a slower rate while others learn at a more rapid rate. In our school system there are gifted students who become impossible students. Their potentials are not being utilized. Underutilisation results in boredom and discipline problems in the school system.

BRAIN DISTURBANCE

Some students are impossible and challenging as a result of inherited disturbance in certain chemicals in the brain's neurotransmitter systems. Students with this defect are inattentive, distractible, impulsive. They don't listen and they don't follow direction. Their school life is a series of failures. Some start out by trying but no matter how hard they try they fail. Constant failure causes them to lose incentive to achieve goals. They become restless and use their restless energy in becoming disciplinary problems.

BEHIND A FACADE OF HILARITY

There are some impossible students who are attention seekers because of their insecurities. Some have failed so many times that they have learnt not to trust their ability. Others degenerate into the class clown so as to hide their failures behind a stance of hilarity. Such students enjoy creating chaos in the classroom. Defiant of authority they enjoy getting teachers angry. Unfortunately, most students admire such students because they break the monotony of what appears to them to be a boring school life.

APATHY

Some impossible students are neither aggressive nor disciplinary problems. They usually come from homes filled with tension and underlying currents of dislike, and frustration. Most children are sensitive to disruptive domestic atmosphere and internalize it. Some apathetic students also come from homes where they are spoilt and pampered. Too much is done for them and too little is demanded of them.

Many teachers have to watch students who have a great deal of potential become apathetic and show callous insensitivity towards those who want to help. These students have a defeatist attitude. They think whatever they do will result in failure. Others just do not care. They view learning and school as a waste of time. They are seriously unmotivated.

"Education is the process not of stuffing people like sausages into a casing but of eliciting from people the potentialities hidden even from themselves".

Sydney Harris

CHAPTER 4

FIGHTING THE PROBLEM

COPING WITH IMPOSSIBLE STUDENTS

Coping with impossible students is a continuous process and begins long before the educator enters the classroom. Classroom management is interrelated with the teachers self-perception and his attitude towards others. His perception of his career as a teacher, his subject area, school, students, principal and colleagues. Does the teacher feel comfortable with himself? Does he bring into the classroom his inferiorities and defences? Does he enter the classroom with the conviction that he is about to teach unlearnable and unteachable students? What kind of relationship does he have with his students?

Classroom control is also contingent on student's respect, appreciation and love for their teachers. Does the educator command a combination of love and respect? Does he know how to take control? Is he conducting himself from a position of strength and nurturing? Does he understand modern day teenagers. Is he capable of communicating effectively with his students? Does he genuinely love the students whom he teaches?

THE POWER OF LOVE

Numerous people have asked me what is the secret of my success with teenagers. How can I change them so easily when parents and significant others seem to fail. I have worked with countless teenagers, some of whom parents gave up on and others whom the education system either discarded or was prepared to discard. I have seem them transformed academically and behaviourally. Some have gone on to higher education.

Their behaviour has never reverted back to the self-destructive patterns and defiance of adult authority that they once exhibited. What is the secret? The formula lies in tough love. The ability to look those youngsters in the eyes and treat them with a combination of empathy, nurturing, strength, gentle guidance, unconditional unflinching love and a no-nonsense attitude that commands respect yet invites friendship and confidentialities. I love these youngsters and they know it and they respond in the most glowing way. I love children, all children. I see their vast potentials. I value them as unique human beings. I believe in them as they believe in me.

No child is born stupid or unlovable. Every child is born in the likeness and image of God. Irrespective of socioeconomic class, race or ethnic origin. Educators must love their students as Christ commanded us to love. True ability to love is to love unconditionally.

Students feel when they are loved or disliked. They are sensitive to environments and feeling states. One does not necessarily have to verbalize feelings and attitudes to them. They sense it. If an educator dislikes his students or a particular student such a student will feel it and may react negatively. Such negative reaction may transcend into disciplinary problems and/or academic lethargy.

If you love a child and is there for that child that child will love and respect you in return. The love of a child is the most enduring, beautiful priceless gift God can give an adult. To feel a child's love is so tender, so rejuvenating. A child feels security, warmth, continuity and transformation in the power of an adult's love. Using all the behavioural ingredients of genuine love and respect, any educator can break the unruly spirit of the impossible student.

Many of today's students come from broken homes. Most of these students are unmotivated to learn. One of the strongest factor which can circumvent the detrimental effect of a broken home is a caring, loving, supportive teacher. Unwritten History is inundated with success stories of students and often the person behind that success has been a teacher.

LESSON PLAN - A MEANS OF CLASSROOM MANAGEMENT

Teachers should plan their work in advance. Have dates and deadlines and classroom routine. Unprepared teachers usually stumble through the class period. Effective lesson preparation reduces uneasiness, frustration, anxiety and classroom unrest.

THE RIGHT TO DISCIPLINE

Some educators give up their right to discipline by constantly passing on the disciplinary problem to the principal. A teacher looks weak, ridiculous and ineffective in the eyes of students by storming out of the classroom and heading for the principal's office. This is a sure way to make students lose respect and create greater classroom chaos. Educators must attempt to deal with problems themselves. In situations where they must consult with the principal, they should do so after school or at the end of the period. A teacher must never appear to pass on his/her power to discipline to someone else.

DO NOT USE FEAR

Some educators attempt to extract obedience and compliance

through fear and intimidation. Fear and intimidation used as deterrents are ineffective for long-term change of behaviour. A student will cease a particular misbehaviour because of the fear of getting into trouble, not because he has internalized the wrongness of the misbehaviour or has developed any sense of responsibility towards himself or others. Consequently, in the absence of the disciplinarian, the student is likely to repeat the misbehaviour or engages constantly in new misbehaviour. Many educators find themselves in a battle to correct constant misbehaviour from the same student.

    HELP
      CREATE
        A
          GOAL
            WITHIN
              THEM

Every student should have a goal. A goal stirs young people on the right course. It keeps the meaning of life in focus; it gives hope and something to work towards.

    A
       GOAL
          GIVES
             THEM
               A
                   PERCEPTION
                   OF
                       THEMSELVES

In relation to the bigger picture.

CHAPTER 5

EFFECTIVE SCHOOL DISCIPLINE

"Discipline is not something that is done to the child; it is something that is done for the child"

Charles Dobson

All schools must have clear guidelines. They must state the consequences which will follow when rules are broken. Rules are best kept when students are active participants in the structuring of these rules and regulations which govern their behaviour. A democratic style of governing will work best with today's Caribbean students. The era when it was demanded of children that they be seen and not heard is over. Television has opened our youngsters to different ways of thinking and different perspectives. A plan of action to help resolve classroom conflict should be drawn with students' active participation.

Students must understand why rules are necessary to govern their behaviour. Students must be given the responsibility of being the watchdog of their own behaviour.

They must clearly understand the school's expectations of them and the rationale behind the rules that govern them so that these rules are not vague generalities.

THE AIM OF DISCIPLINE IN CARIBBEAN SCHOOLS

The aim of discipline should be as a learning process whereby:

1. The students would develop a sense of responsibility towards himself/herself and others.
2. Should develop profound understanding of the kind of behaviours which are deemed acceptable.
3. Should internalize the value of the discipline so as to produce a maturity which will result in control of character.
4. Discipline must be built on a relationship of mutual respect and trust and promote a positive image of authority.
5. Praise and reward serve to reinforce desirable behaviour.

EFFECTIVE SCHOOL COUNSELLING A PREVENTATIVE TOOL TO MISBEHAVIOUR

An efficient and effectively operated guidance counselling department involves not only the duties of the guidance coun-

sellor but also that of a school psychologist and psychometrist. Students bring numerous problems into the classroom. A student's lack of aspiration, poor academic response, socially maladjusted behaviour are dependent on a number of pertinent factors such as:
- Perceptual and maturational development.
- Value system, mode of discipline within the home attitude, emotional development.
- Psychological factors such as intense level of anxiety, irrational fears, depression, obsessive/compulsive behaviour etc.
- Eating habits. Diet.
- Neurologic deficits such as Attention Deficit/Hyperactivity disorder. Central language dysfunction.
- Developmental phase during adolescence-hormonal imbalance.
- Peer pressure.
- Physiological symptomatic reactions such as obesity.
- Sexual molestation (experienced).
- Incest (experienced)
- Disesteemed learners, i.e. students who perform poorly in school tasks but are not learning-disabled, mentally handicapped or emotionally disturbed.

These students fail in school for a variety of reasons. Many factors within the student work like the mechanism of a clock. A faulty mechanism may and often does result in the breakdown of the machine. For example, a student who is perceptually underdeveloped will exhibit physical and mental lassitude which will create poor academic response. Poor academic response might create frustration which may create classroom disruption.

To use another example, a student may have high academic ability, however the home environment may not be conducive to proper discipline. Domestic problems may transcend into how the student views him/herself and others. The student's perception may transcend into his or her attitude towards school, teachers, education, aspiration and future career.

Facing the need of students mean utilizing the resources of an appropriate specialist so that guidance counselling can therefore be in direct response to:

1. The source of the inappropriate behaviour
2. Towards the behaviour
3. Towards modification or eradication of the problem behaviour.

SUCCESSFUL CLASSROOM MANAGEMENT FORMAT

Problem students should be placed into two categories:

1. Low risk students.
2. High risk students.

Criteria for placement
(a) Level of classroom/homework response.
(b) Severity of inappropriate social behaviour within the school/home environment
(c) Motoric/perceptual developmental lag.
(d) Degree of emotional maladjustment

Note: An identification check-list will be used as guideline by teachers.

Phase I
When faced with problem student, the teacher fills out a referral form.

Note: Forms for all low risk students are to be filled out and signed by the referring teacher, however, with regards to high risk students, the following steps must be followed:
(a) Teacher fills out a referral form.
(b) Sends the student with the form to the Principal who examines the problem and signs the form.

Phase II
The problem student is sent to the counselling department with signed form. All referred students must be accompanied by a signed form and a correct behaviour plan slip.

Phase III

The counsellor evaluates the problem student. If the student falls into the Low Risk Category, counselling is administered and the Correct Behaviour Plan (CBP) and Daily Report Card becomes operative.

If the student falls into the High Risk Category he or she enters into Phase IV for psychometric testing and intensive psychological evaluation and treatment.

Phase IV

The problem student undertakes a battery of paper/pencil and drawing tests. A confidential report is then issued concerning the findings of testing as well as implications for instructions and treatment.

Parent(s) and Guardian(s) will be contacted by telephone. Psychological findings will be made immediately available to the relevant parent(s)/guardian(s) and if necessary his/her/(their) active participation (in therapy sessions) sought.

If the problem is due to a developmental lag (hearing, vision etc.) referrals will be made to medical personnel for further evaluation.

Phase V

Therapy is administered. The problem student is kept on file for further review of the case until a marked improvement is seen in his or her behaviour.

Phase VI
After modification of undesirable behaviour, counselling/therapy will terminate after two months (unless unacceptable behaviour reoccurs shortly thereafter).

Phase VII
Follow-up in the form of additional assessment or review of progress will be made after the two months interval following initial diagnosis and treatment. If the student continues to show marked improvement in academic and social behaviour his or her file will become inactive.

IDENTIFICATION CHECK LIST FOR HIGH RISK STUDDENTS

External personality traits and behavioural tendencies used as measuring devices in the referral of students for initial assessment, compilation of personality profile, psychometric evaluation, counselling, guidance and/or psychotherapy.

1. Students who cause consistent disciplinary problem.
2. Students who display erratic behaviour patterns. (behaviour which appears suspiciously abnormal)
3. Excessive truancy.
4. Low frustration tolerance. (easily frustrated)

5. Drug users.
6. Students who display habitual listlessness.
7. Students who consistently hint on suicidal tendencies.
8. Students who have little or no aspirations.
9. Students who exhibit poor social behaviour in class (e.g. withdrawal tendencies, abnormal degree of shyness).
10. Students who have low attention span. (Mind constantly wanders while lesson is in progress).
11. Students who suffer from emotional difficulties.
12. Students who loiter on the school premises (after school) and seem reluctant to go home. (This must be a constant behaviour trait).
13. Students who habitually break most of the school rules. (With special emphasis on blatant disregard for dress code).
14. Students who display abnormal degrees of hyper-activity. (Can't keep still for any recognizable length of time).
15. Students who display excessive degrees of aggression (in attitude - verbal or physical - engagement in constant fights).

16. Students who exhibit any other serious behavioural problem not speficied above.

****

Please note: Students who exhibit the above-outlined personality/behavioural traits are the ones most likely to cause classroom disruption, show little or no regard for authority and have a low academic record.

CHECK LIST FOR LOW RISK STUDENTS

External personality traits and behavioural tendencies used as measuring devices in the referral of students for initial assessment, psychometric evaluation, guidance-counselling and/or psychotherapy.

1. Underachievers (students who work below their intellectual capabilities).
2. Overachievers (students who display an abnormal degree of anxiety that he or she achieves high grades at all times. Failure is viewed as a personality deficit).
3. Students who stutter. (Stuttering may not be a neurologic handicap but stems from excessive anxiety and high levels of stress).
4. Students who are developed physically more than the average physical development of the class with

special emphasis on students in the 1st to 3rd Forms.
5. Truancy
6. Students who are physically underdeveloped than the average physical development of the class (with special emphasis on male students in the 4th and 5th Forms).
7. Students who are older than the average age of the class. (Greater emphasis on girls in the lower Forms).
8. Students who consistently do not do their homework.
9. Students who have been held back.
10. Students who are obese or simply overweight.
11. Suspected victims of ADD (Attention Deficit Disorder).

INTRODUCTION OF IN-SCHOOL SUSPENSION (ISS) TO ADDRESS PROBLEMS BEHAVIOUR

1. The student is told:
    (a) what he or she does well.
    (b) what behaviour will not be tolerated in the classroom
    (c) How such behaviour will be addressed.
2. When the student engages in a problem behaviour, the

EFFECTIVE SCHOOL DISCIPLINE

teacher tells him or her what the behaviour is, that it is unacceptable and that this is a warning.
3. If the student ceases the misbehaviour, he or she may remain in the class.
4. If the student continues or repeats the behaviour, or begins another misbehaviour, the teacher tells him or her to report to In-School -Suspension (ISS). (A special room designated for that purpose) and gives him or her a correct behaviour plan (CBP).
5. On receiving a CBP slip the student leaves the room without argument and reports to ISS. Should the student refuse to leave the room, the teacher sends another student to bring the Principal to remove the student from the room.
6. At In-School-Suspension, the student writes (on the CBP) a plan for correcting his or her misbehaviour. The counsellor or Discipline Head may assist him or her with this plan if necessary.
7. Any concern or reservations the student has about the classroom teacher's action in sending him or her to ISS are discussed by him or her with the Principal, Counsellors or Discipline Head only. No arguments must be made to the teacher.

8. The completed and approved CBP is signed by the students and the educator in charge. The student is then given a daily report card. The daily report card is the student's pass back to class.
9. Classroom or subject teachers encourage any positive behaviour by telling the students exactly what the behaviour is, and that they approve of it, this is done as frequently as possible (aim for at least one positive comment per class. Such comments would include successful fulfilment of the correct behaviour plan.

DAILY REPORT

1. The problem student carries a daily report card and takes to the subject teacher after each period.
2. Brings card to guidance counsellors each day, then home to parents/guardian who signs and help monitor homework.
3. Teachers make all entries, i.e. homework assignment and signs or initials it.
4. At the end of the week the form is taken to the Principal who examines it and signs it.
5. The form is then returned to the counsellor or discipline Head. If scores reveal that behaviour/attitude and/or homework response have not shown a marked improve-

ment, the student's parent(s) or guardian will be called in for an interview.

Daily report and counselling will be terminated after 2-3 weeks positive entries.

GLASSER'S REALITY THERAPY - AN EFFECTIVE DISCIPLINE TOOL

The success of Glasser's reality therapy rests in the utilization of a self-interest philosophy. It takes the interest of the student into account.

The student enters into a contract with himself - a contract for success - he assumes responsibility for his own future success and behaviour.

The teacher is not critical but supportive. The student writes his plan for success and begins to act on these plans.

Consequences for failing to follow the plan are laid out and the consequences are set if the contract is broken. The teacher supports the student in his/her effort at success.

CORRECT BEHAVIOUR PLAN

My incorrect behaviour was:	My plan to correct this behaviour is:

_____	_____

TEACHER'S FOLLOW-UP	....

....	Signature of Student

Date:...............................	Date:...............................

COUNSELLING

1. The counsellor keeps the CBP slip and remind the student(s) (at the beginning of the day) of his/her (their) contractual agreement.
2. Failure to fulfill a CBP is discussed with the student by the educator in charge. The teacher concerned may be invited to a relevant counselling session but discussion of failed CBP PLAN <u>should not under any circumstances</u> occur in the classroom. The counselling session focusses on the disciplinary issues only. The In-School-Suspension (ISS) behavioural modification plan is used for problems of a disciplinary nature. Any other appointments the students has with the counsellor are to be scheduled outside of a disciplinary context.

N.B. The CBP is a contractual agreement between the student and the discipline Head of the school.

Aim

1. To develop within the student a sense of responsibility for the portrayal of negative/positive behaviours and attitudes.
2. Elimination of the placement of blame (guilt) unto someone else for inappropriate behaviours/attitudes.

3. Reawakening or development of moral self.
4. Fostering of self-discipline and a sense of responsibility towards others.
5. Modification of inappropriate behaviour/attitudes.

PREVENTING INAPPROPRIATE BEHAVIOUR

The merit system

The establishment of a positive reward (merit) system would serve to communicate expectation, reinforce, encourage and maintain appropriate classroom behaviour and attitude and give misbehaving students an opportunity to gain teachers and peers confidence and respect. It serves as a venue for cleaning the slate of misbehaviour.

The following are the criteria for the awarding of merits:

(a) Good work, effort, special cooperation in school affairs, excellent classroom, homework response, etc.

(b) The introduction of a merit competition. This competition may be run into section (for example 5 section). One section for each year (Form) group. Classes compete with each other. Winning classes or individual winners will be announced by the Principal at assembly. Appropriate awards or incentives given (e.g. merit certificates, winning class allowed to come to school on the Friday in "dress" clothes or leave school 20 minutes earlier on a Friday etc.) Criteria should serve for the awarding of merits to encourage responsible behaviour, activity, good dress code, academic excellence and improvement, comportment, decorum, helpfulness and so on.

Demerit system

Be precise about which punishment will be met with which offense, i.e. which offense will be met by one demerit, two demerits, etc.

e.g. Demerits are given for the following reasons:
- Being late for a lesson
- Coming to a lesson without proper books and equipment
- Wearing incorrect uniform
- Unnecessary talking during assembly
- Two demerits for "bad" language
- Three demerits for being out of the school property etc.

during school hours.

Detention

A student receiving 4 demerits in a week will be placed in detention; 8 demerits will lead to 2 detentions and so on.

N.B. Number of demerits are left to the discretion of the Principal or disciplinary committee.

Any student failing to attend a detention will be sent home until parents come in to school.

A student who is guilty of a more serious offence other than those listed under demerits could be given a dention (without first receiving demerits), suspension, corporal punishment etc.

The Discipline Book

Step 1

Year (Form) Heads are selected from among members of staff by the Principal,

OR

The Disciplinary Committee could become an ongoing active machinery.

Step 2

Various classes may be placed under the direct "disciplinary jurisdiction" of the Year Heads or individual members of the Disciplinary Committee or Year Head could be responsible for the 4th and 5th Forms; another for the 3rd Form and another for the 1st and 2nd Forms.

Step 3

If a teacher has a problem student whom she cannot deal with, the student will be entered into the Discipline Book and sent to the appropriate Year Head or member of the Disciplinary Committee.

Step 4

Year Heads or members of the Disciplinary Committee are responsible for examining the Discipline Book daily.

N.B. Teachers would be responsible for their own discipline (except corporal punishment and suspension) but once teachers have entered the names of students in the Discipline Book, they can no longer dictate what type of punishment should be meted out to students.

The Year Head or Disciplinary Committee can determine what type of punishment should be given to students, for example, detention, corporal punishment, "community work", odd jobs around the school, etc. in other words, a punishment to fit the crime or recommendation for counselling, or the handling of the offence by the Principal.

N.B. The Principal retains the sole authority at all times to implement corporal punishment and suspension.

EFFECTIVE SCHOOL DISCIPLINE

Advantages in having a discipline book

The Discipline Book is good for record keeping because when a parent is called in for a conference, the parent can see for herself how many offences have been committed by the student/their child. Thus, the Discipline Book can also act as a safeguard for teachers.

The Discipline Book also filters out a lot of unnecessary petty discipline problems that can be handled by the teacher. It will not only record how many times students are entered in the Book but also shows frequency of teachers who enter a student or students.

The frequency of entry of a particular student could indicate that the student needs special attention. The Discipline Book is also a cooling off period. Once the teacher has to enter the name of the student and offence, it could offer a chance to allow the teacher to re-assess the incident.

Format of the Discipline Book

| Date | Form | Student | Offence | Action Taken | Signature of Head or member of D.C |

CHAPTER 6

BETTER STUDENT-TEACHER RELATIONSHIP

PROMOTING BETTER STUDENT-TEACHER RELATIONSHIP

"Teen talk"... A student's recommendation

Asked what factors would facilitate better student-teacher relationship, Talitta, a Fifth Former, quickly pointed out TEEN TALK. "Set an hour aside each week for teen talk," Talitta explained. "This is one of the healthiest things any school can do for itself. Have a weekly discussion with students. Give them an outlet in which to air their grievances. Students' grievances should be taken seriously. Together with the students, the teachers should find workable solutions," continued Talitta. "Teachers should hold discussion on various topics which interest students. During discussions they could encourage the shyer students to participate so that everyone's opinion can be heard. Each student will feel important". Talitta was careful to emphasize that the major success for teen talk rests in the students' interest in it. "They must want to be part of it and it must not be seen as something that is boring, a total waste of time or something that is thrust on them".

"Selection of the teacher/coordinator is vital," said Talitta. When asked to highlight certain characteristics of the coordinator, she replied that a nurturing disposition, genuine love for children as well as the ability to listen was vital for the success of teen talk.

"Teen Talk must be viewed both by students and teachers as a time allotted to them - the student (their own special time) when their needs and wants would be taken seriously."

"It must be viewed as a creation for opportunities for involving students in making decisions that will affect them. Teen Talk must not be dominated by teachers.

"Students jointly with staff members can work on solutions to problems which affect the learning environment. It can be used as an avenue for building the groups' self-esteem." concluded this fifth former.

Teen Talk

Teen Talk will also serve as a preventative measure to maladaptive classroom behaviours and poor academic response.These discussions will sensitize students to community awareness, career opportunities, goal setting, sound moral values and so on.

Some topics for discussion during Teen Talk are:
1. School discipline and its function in relation to the student's development of moral self and social conscience.
2. The importance of education and how it relate to one's future development, i.e. job career, socio-economic and professional status etc.
3. Sexual misconduct/irresponsible sexual behaviour pre mature/teenage pregnancy and social diseases with special emhasis on AIDS.
4. Legal and illegal drugs. Their harmful effect on the adolescent boy or girl's physical growth, mental capacity and competence, future capacity for procreation, behaviour, learning, attitude, etc.
5. The family, value systems and its interrelationship to the student's self-concept, social self, behaviour, attitude.
6. Teaching on moral values.
7. Diet, exercise, the food we eat and how it relates to excess weight, learning, behaviour, mood swing.
8. Student's everyday proficiencies of self-care in such areas as good eating habits, proper dress codes.
9. Acceptance of social responsibilities.

BETTER STUDENT-TEACHER RELATIONSHIP

10. The importance of effective communication.
11. Sexuality, biological development, sexual responsibilities, self-respect, sexual misconceptions. The key factors motivating the West Indian male's sexual drive.
12. Teenage pregnancy and its negative impact on physical maturity, career opportunities, marketing skills, reputation, etc.
13. Careers and their significance to the Caribbean's economic structure. How the student's present choices may affect his or her future socio-economic development.
14. The value of mistakes/failures. In some students, academic failures often develop into a defeatest attitude which only compounds the problems, i.e. failure leads to more failure. Discussion will focus on the fact that failure is often a motivator to learning. Focus on solution rather than on self-blame.
15. Other topics; self-esteem, self-confidence, faith, courage perseverance, etc. Divorce/separation and so on.
    <u>Theme for the week:</u> At the end of each discussion the students are given a theme which they will reflect on for the week.

Personality Development Club may be a branch of Teen Talk focus should be on the development of a positive personality, and role play so as to develop empathy with parents and teachers. Development of self-esteem, self-confidence. The inclusion of strategy games: to help students develop judgment and planning abilities.
Breathing exercise: Aim at stress reduction, anxiety reduction.

HOW STUDENTS VIEW THEIR TEACHERS

Students place teachers into neat little single worded categories. These categories are based on the teacher's attitude, behaviour, teaching style, classroom management, relationship with students and their peers perception of that teacher.

We hear such labels as "mean, lazy, boring, unfair, stupid, strict, nice, friendly and so on". These labels might not realistically apply to a teacher, however, it is the student's perception and they arrange their behaviour, attitude, response style based on these labels.

The mature and smart educator will want to know his or her students perception, without being judgmental or vindictive. For some educators, this is going to be very difficult to do because most of us perceive ourselves differently from the way others perceive us but it may help if educators bear in mind that students are not judgmental they simply judge teachers and they see character flaws that the average adult refuses to believe or see in him or herself.

Tammy a Fourth Former feels that a key factor in the promotion of better teacher-student relationship is the fact that "teachers must know how students see them and what we expect from them"

What students look for in their teachers

What are students expectations of their teachers?
The following response have been complied from questionnaires that were disseminated among hundreds of students:
- Concise and to the point lessons. Many students do not like their teachers straying to different topics.
- Students look for special qualities in each teacher. Qualities that they can feel comfortable with and relate to easily.
- Their teachers must be there for them, to help guide them when they are faced with personal difficulties. They want to be listened to.
- They want their teachers to create a learning environment free from chaos. A learning environment that is conducive to structure and organization.
Teaching style must be both enthusiastic and resourceful.

- Students want teachers to love and respect them as intelligent worthwhile human beings. they want their feelings and opinions to be taken into consideration.
- If they do not understand a concept, their teachers must not be too busy to explain it.
- Teachers must be understanding, patient and not be critical and condemning of their academic mistakes.
- Students want their teachers to act as grown-ups and not teenagers. Some teachers in a desperate attempt to be accepted use slangs and "try to be cool".
- Teachers must be able to maintain classroom control. This is perhaps the most important teacher trait that students respect.
- Students want their teachers to listen to them more.
- They do not respect teachers who feel they know everything.
- They do not like lethargic, insensitive, defensive and insecure teachers
- Students want their teachers to relate to them like feeling human beings. They want them to respect understand empathize with them. They also believe that the ideal teacher is fair-minded. They must not show preference to one student as compared to anothers.

BETTER STUDENT-TEACHER RELATIONSHIP

- Their teacher must be well groomed.
- They must know their subjects; they must be prepared at all times. Students are not fooled; they know when teachers do not know their subject matter or are unprepared. They are merciless and harsh in their criticism.
- They do not want their teachers to undermine other teachers. Some teachers become literally afraid of their classroom. To create as minimal stress as possible in their work life, there are those who attempt to curry favour with students by undermining other teachers. Although some students regard these teachers as nice, nice is often used loosely and vague - In reality they hold little or no respect for such educators.
- Some educators make excuses for their mistakes or try to cover it up with a stance of self-righteousness.

One of the most effective ways of gaining students' trust and respect is to readily admit error when it is pointed out. When errors are obvious to students and it is denied, the teacher diminishes him/herself in their students eyes. The ability to admit to one's error is a sure sign of maturity.

A student's perception

Talitta believes it is also imperative for teachers to understand the reasons why students give trouble. "Remember we are going through a transitory period. We are not children, neither are we adults." She explains "we want adults to guide us but we want to be given sufficient space in which to make decisions which affects our lives. We no longer accept blindly everything that is said to us. We question your love and judgment. We begin to find that you are not perfect, that you make mistakes. We resent you adults for that because you are so judgmental when it comes to us teenagers. You adults say to us, 'do this and do that' but the values which you try to give us is contrary to what you practise. We stop trusting and stop listening".

"You must realize that some teenagers come from hostile environments where fighting and misbehaviour is a way of survival, and they bring the habit into the classroom".

"You know we get extremely frustrated when we try to please adults but they criticise us so much that we begin to feel that we can't do anything right. So why try at all?"

"Some students have such an inferiority complex" she continued, "adults have no idea what it's like to struggle with an inferiority complex. To want to be accepted so desperately.

Some of us want to be accepted by our peers so we misbehave just to be applauded by our peers and become a member of the in-group. I know it's not a cool thing to do but nevertheless some students do it".

"I am sure it would surprise you to know that some teenagers cause trouble and do badly at school as a means of revenge against parent or parents. This is dumb because in the final analysis the teenager is only hurting him or herself but they do not regard it like that."

"The desire to avoid failure is a strong point why some teenagers misbehave in school. Some teenagers are so frightened by failure that they cause trouble. The rational behind this weird behaviour is that if they fail they will have an excuse for their failure. Some of us are so afraid of messing up our lives that we mess it up anyway, "Talitta concluded.

Tammy believes that if teachers can look at themselves honestly and assume some of the blame for classroom disruption, this would be beneficial in better teacher-student relationship.

CHAPTER 7

THE SUCCESSFUL TEACHER

THE MOST SUCCESSFUL TEACHER
Like parents the most successful teachers are "those who have skills to get behind the eyes of the child, seeing what he sees, thinking what he thinks, feeling what he feels."

James Dobson

"Seeing what he sees" **DEVELOPING EMPATHY**

Developing empathy means being able to walk in the other person's shoes. Knowing, feeling, understanding, anticipating the student's reaction. Having a general idea of their environment will give the teacher an idea of their needs, moods, fears and attitudes.

Such knowledge will act as a power valve for the educator. The student's behaviour and reaction will be placed in perspective and make handling such a student easier.

Keep in mind that "Youth have exalted notions because they

have not yet been humbled in life. They love too much, they hate too much, they think they know everything; that is why they overdo everything."

Aristotle

WHEN YOU WERE YOUNG YOU TOO SAID FOOLISH THINGS, DID FOOLISH THINGS, THOUGHT FOOLISH THOUGHTS BUT IN THE END YOU TURNED OUT ALRIGHT.

FOURTEEN COMMANDMENTS FOR TEACHERS

You are a teacher because you care, you care because you are a teacher.

1. Stay calm under pressure. Screaming, throwing temper tantrums are ineffective means of classroom management.
2. Do not take student's misbehaviour as a personal affront.
3. Do not pass on your right to discipline to the Principal. If you do, your student will view you as weak and ineffective.
4. Do not allow yourself to get trapped in a power struggle with your impossible students.

5. Have a positive attitude towards yourself at all times.
6. If you are experiencing difficulties, talk to other teachers whom you trust about your difficulties.
7. Exercise fairness. Youngsters have a keen sense of justice. Nothing makes a student dislike or disrespect an educator more than the perception that they are being unfair.
8. Believe in the intelligence and potential of every student.
9. Discipline with fairness and consistency.
10. Never engage in personality conflicts with your students.
11. Love each student as if they were your biological child.
12. Bear in mind that God has placed each student in your hands to mould and nurture.
13. Your task as a teacher is a noble one.
14. You, more than any other adult has the power to effect changes in your students.

BE CAREFUL OF RASH JUDGMENTS

"I was kicked out of school in Third Form, " pointed out a 24 year old labourer.

"The school counsellor and the Headmaster were convinced I was on drugs. They expelled me. I wish I had a good education. If I did I would not be where I am today".

The Headmaster and school counsellor were convinced he

was on drugs because he was quiet and had blood shot eyes. Be careful of rash judgments. Your actions might destroy a child's future.

CHAPTER 8

CHILDREN CAN LEARN IN INSTRUCTIONAL SUCCESSFUL SCHOOLS

The following are essential criteria for instructional schools:

1. **A goal and commitment**

Every successful school has a goal and a sense of commitment to its student body. It's plans, organization, activities, resources and energy are focussed upon its goals.

2. **A strong Principal**

Strong effective principals make good schools. Principals must have the courage of conviction to put the school's goal into effect. They must be willing to take bold steps to create homogeneity among students and staff members. They must be the watchdog of classroom management and must practise fairness, firmness, and integrity in their dealings with the student and staff bodies. Principals of successful schools are supportive of progressive initiatives of staff members. They are totally involved in their educational environment.

3. Providing a learning climate aimed to produce successful students

Successful schools provide a positive learning climate where staff members cooperate and work steadily towards the goals of the school.

4. Belief in students

Every successful school believes in the ability of every student. Their response, expectations and other positive factors or of inter-relationship reflect that belief.

Successful schools do not succumb to the misguided philosophy that some students are born inherently stupid. The child who does not have a brain defect has high academic ability.

5. Consistent interest

Consistent interest in students' performance and the monitoring of their academic activities make successful schools successful.

6. High level of parent involvement

Parent involvement in their children's educational community helps generate a learning attitude in their youngsters. Teacher-parent cooperation provides a silent strong support system for students. It is one of the strongest hallmarks of a successful school.

Case Study
A school, a principal, a teacher, a psychologist and an experiment.

A School
Antigua Girls' High School
Throughout the years, Antigua Girls High School has maintained its position as the leading school in Antigua and Barbuda, whereas some schools have had to resort to "artificial levels of success" i.e. entrants for the CXC examinations are streamlined. (These schools concentrate only on a handful of students who are performing at capacity level). Antigua Girls High School continues to achieve high level of academic passes from its student body. Its student body comprises:
1. High achievers, i.e. entrants who were high performers at the primary level.
2. Average and low achievers, i.e. unmotivated students and those who were outperformed at the primary level.
3. Students performing at an average and below average levels who were transferred from a private girls high school.

Antigua Girls High School has transformed these transferred students into excellent, confident and highly motivated students. What is the secret of this school's tremendous success? There is an old adage which claims that a school is its principal and staff members.

A Principal

Mrs. Violet Lewis, a former Principal of the Antigua Girls High School and now Chief Education Officer in the Ministry of Education, offered strong leadership to the school during her years of tenure. This was reflected in her policies and behaviour and leadership style. Mrs Lewis a highly intelligent, courageous and wise woman who has tremendous discernment ability and humanity, a woman of independent thinking. She is not swayed by the opinions of others but listens and weighs the evidence carefully before making decisions. Her intellectual capacity, strength and character, humanity and sense of fair play have worked to promote consensus among her staff members and a warm atmosphere among her student body.

What struck one forcefully about this remarkable Principal was the atmosphere of parenthood she exuded. One got the impression that she was not only an educator but a friend and a parent... her student's parent. Doubtlessly, she took her job of caretaker, friend, and educator seriously. She understood her students, their feelings, idiosyncrasies and moods and was there for them. Antigua Girls High School under her able leadership portrayed a uniformity of professional teaching techniques, goals and behaviour towards students. A detailed analysis of interrelationship of staff and students indicated that under her leadership the school exuded a non-threatening atmosphere. Staff enthusiasm, belief in students' ability, tough love and a consistent nurturing atmosphere acted as intrinsic motivation and regulated the academic and social behaviour of the students in a positive avenue.

A teacher

Miss Richards is currently the POB (Principles of Business) teacher at Antigua Girls High School. She is well-loved and respected by her students. All her students aim high and usually pass with distinction. In the 1996 CXC results for Principles of Business out of a total of 47 students, 38 of her students achieved "A" (Ones) and 9 students achieved "B" (Twos). Each succeeding year her students achieve an incredible amount of honour passes.

Miss Richards has high expectations for her students and she lets them know this through her actions, attitude and verbalization. She loves and respect her students and her belief in them is translated in their classroom behaviour and outstanding academic record.

Among her students she is regarded as friendly and warm. "Someone who explains things to us, is real nice; we just like her, she is a good teacher."

Her students speak of her with genuine warmth and love. Miss Richards engages in harmless little chit-chats with them, little curiosities and inquiries at appropriate times. She establishes an emotional bond with her students. She treats them like human beings and not academic robots. When asked about her classroom management style, her students had this to say about her: "Most of us don't give her trouble; we like her. Why should we give her trouble? Furthermore, she makes the lessons interesting".

A psychologist and an experiment

"Uncontrolled and noisy classrooms ruled by bullies determined to disturb the concentration of the few industrious students".

"Teacher disillusionment, conflict and a high level of incompetence among staff members were predominant factors in this school. There was widespread lack of cooperation, backstabbing of teachers by other teachers in the presence of and to students. The few staff members who showed interest in their educational community were regarded with suspicion and seen as threats to the status quo. There was also tremendous diversity in classroom management. The classes which were better managed were being disturbed by the disciplinary laxity of others.

The Principal, although a wonderful person, offered a chaotic brand of leadership in both educational policies and interpersonal relationship. His leadership style plummeted his staff into unnecessary conflict, consequently, there was widespread unacceptance of his proposed policies. In terms of adult leadership, there was an absence of real leadership. The school was on "automatic pilot". The leadership of the school had been taken over by a small gang of bullying male students". Excerpts from a journal (Dr. B. Merrill - 1994) chronicling a disruptive school in Antigua.

An experiment

The situation was approached from the standpoint of:

1. The philosophy that the effective reduction of behaviour of bullying students meant better classroom management and

2. A strong brand of leadership meant a better school

Effective measures initiated

* Leadership visibility was established.

* Assessment of the school climate, staff members, personality profile and leadership skills of Principal, interpersonal relationship between staff members, relationship between Principal and staff, relationship between educators and students, communication level between parents and educators, students' perception of school and staff's perception of Principal and

school were made.
Handling the problem
Bullying students were targeted and isolated from the mainstream of the school for approximately two months or when behaviour improved. The concept of I.S.S. and Daily Report Record Card was initiated. These proved to be effective disciplinary tools. It was important to break the unruly spirit of these students if the control of the school was to be wrestled from them.

A divide and conquer strategy was employed. The cooperation of the rest of the student body was sought by explaining to them the detrimental effect the bullying students' behaviour was having on their progress and their future. Their perception of these students was changed from one of admiration and intimidation to non-acceptance. The bullying students' behaviour and not the students were seen as the enemy.

Reducing Disruptive Behaviours
A number of tools were used as measures aimed at reducing disruptive behaviours.

* Inappropriate behaviours were dealt with immediately and swiftly while positive behaviours were reinforced.
* The cooperation of parents were sought. The import-

ance of rules for the children was highlighted with calm rationality. Their sense of parenthood was appealed to.
* A non-threatening learning environment was created where the students actually looked forward to the learning period."
* Sensitivity to the feeling - tones of the students was a predominant factor in dealing with them.
* When the occasion presented itself, harmless jokes were given and encouraged. This tended to diffuse tension and create emotional bonding.
* Students were encouraged to verbalize ideas. This resulted in the development of a sense of importance.
* Because teenagers resent being ordered, emphasis was placed on direction giving. Teenagers comply better when their cooperation is sought.
* A democratic style of relationship was entered into where appropriate; at other times, it was vital to be autocratic. This strategy proved extremely effective in exercising mutual respect, the development of friendship and in changing unacceptable behaviour to acceptable.
* A positive relationship with the students" parents was established. Good communication with parents is crucial to students' attitude to the educational environment.

* Emphasis was placed on creating stimulating lectures delivered in a warm and friendly atmosphere.
* A humanistic approach was taken at all times with a high level of verbal activity from the students.
* The class cooperation and input was sought in establishing principles of conduct. This helped greatly in avoiding situations conducive to troublesome behaviour.

The bullying students

Isolation, I.S.S. Daily Report Card, a consistent policy of force, tough love, psychological counselling, belief and concern for these students' welfare, praise and encouragement of good behaviour helped eventually to erode their tough shell of aggression. They melted into the normal pattern of school. Leadership of the school had been regained. It was on its way upwards and forward.

A final word
about..............

............the importance of Parents Involvement.

CHAPTER 9

Parent's Involvement

Parents must not release their parental responsibilities into the hands of the school. They must assume their primary responsibility to their children. In the promotion of proper classroom behaviour and good academic response, parent-school cooperation is essential.

There are a number of ways that parents can help their children perform better at school. Parental consistent involvement and support are key factors in helping children do better at school.

Some do's and don't's for parents
- Visit your child's school.
- Attend P.T.A. meetings.
- Show interest in your child's schoolwork and school activities.
- Ask questions.
- Support your child's school.
- Do not speak derogatorily about your child's teacher, Principal and school, especially in the presence of your

child.
- Do not be confrontational or judgmental to teacher (it is essential that you avoid doing so in the presence of your child or other students).
- Talk and listen to your child's teacher. Mutually, civil communication is more effective.
- Find out who your child's friends are.
- Listen to the complaints of your child but do not be too quick to take sides.
- Provide firm, loving discipline. **UNDISCIPLINED MINDS CANNOT LEARN.**

DAILY REPORT CARD

Name of Student ....

Form ....

Form Teacher ....

Please comment on student's behaviour and academic response by indicating

good (**g**)   average (**a**)   poor (**p**)   in the space provided;

Under the headings: Academic Behaviour (**B**)   Academic Response (**R**)   Subject Teacher's initials (**T.I.**)

Days of the week	Period I Comments			Period II Comments			Period III Comments			Period IV Comments			Period V Comments			Period VI Comments			Period VII Comments			Period VIII Comments		
	B	R	T.I.	B	R	T.I.	B	R	T.I.	B	R	T.I.	B	R	T.I.	B	R	T.I.	B	R	T.I.	B	R	T.I.
Mon																								
Tue																								
Wed																								
Thu																								
Fri																								

© Dr. Beverly Merrill, 1997